Time Time Travel

Helen Chapman

Contents

Meet the Time Travel Twins

Hi! We are David and Sara, the Time Travel Twins.
We can go back in time.
First stop, the Stone Age!

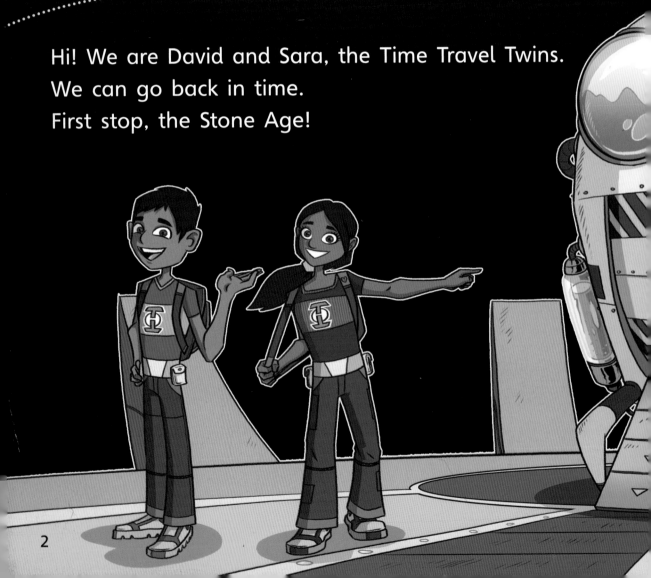

Places we will go:

Italy

China

Egypt

People of
The Stone Age

In the Stone Age, people made tools from stone. They ate animals, plants and berries. They knew how to make fire.

Stone Age tool

Stone Age people cooking food

The people of the Stone Age made paintings on the walls of their caves.

An ancient cave painting

The people of the Stone Age wore
animal fur when it was cold.

STONE AGE PEOPLE:

David: Stone Age people hunted animals for food and fur.

Sara: They also picked berries, plant roots and fruit.

David: Yes, and they invented tools.

Now let's meet the Egyptians.

The Ancient Egyptians

In their writing, the Ancient Egyptians used pictures of real things, like a bird or an eye.

Egyptian writing is called hieroglyphics (say *hi-ra-gli-fiks*).

The Egyptians also built huge **pyramids** and **statues**. The statue below has the body of a lion and the head of a king.

It took over **80** years to build some of the pyramids.

This statue is called the Great Sphinx.

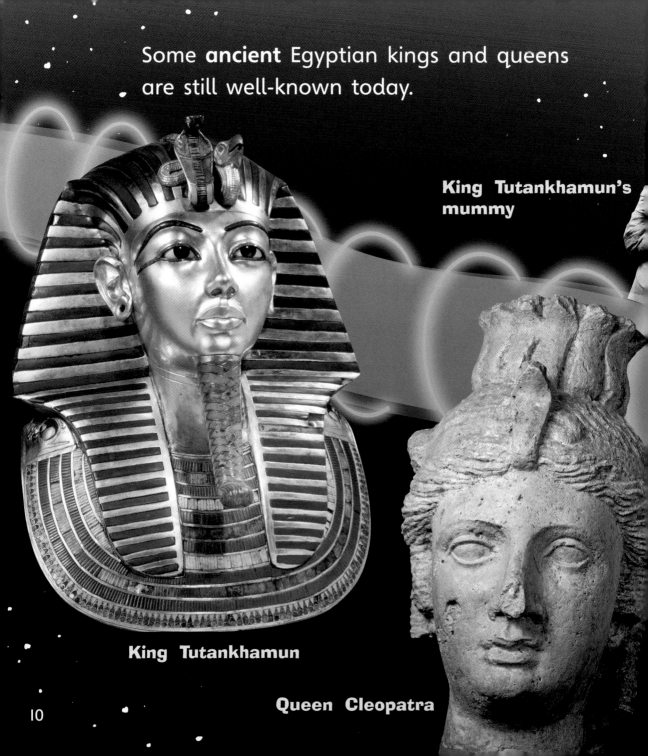

Some **ancient** Egyptian kings and queens are still well-known today.

King Tutankhamun's mummy

King Tutankhamun

Queen Cleopatra

THE KING OF EGYPT

David: Tutankhamun was King of Egypt when he was only nine. How cool is that?

Sara: But he died when he was 18 and was turned into a **mummy**.

David: Not so cool!

Time to go to Ancient China!

Ancient China

The ancient Chinese **invented** lots of great things:

- paper
- the **compass**
- fireworks.

fireworks

a very old Chinese compass

a Chinese paper scroll

The Chinese had fantastic writing, too.
They invited a printing press and made books!

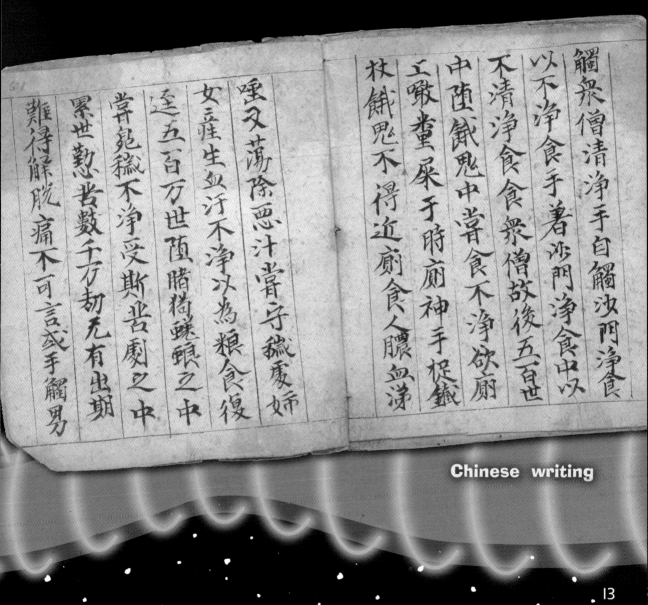

Chinese writing

The ancient Chinese built a huge wall to keep China safe from other countries. It is called the Great Wall of China.

The Great Wall of China is over 6000 kilometres long.

THE GREAT WALL OF CHINA

David: Quick! Get building.

Sara: Why?

David: We've got to keep China safe.

Sara: But it took 1700 years to make the wall.

David: I didn't say it would be quick!

Time to go! Next stop, Europe!

15

The Romans

The Roman army was very strong. They went to war to win other lands.

A ROMAN GLADIATOR

David: I wish I was a **gladiator** ...

Sara: Some gladiators had to fight to the death.

David: They did? I'm out of here!

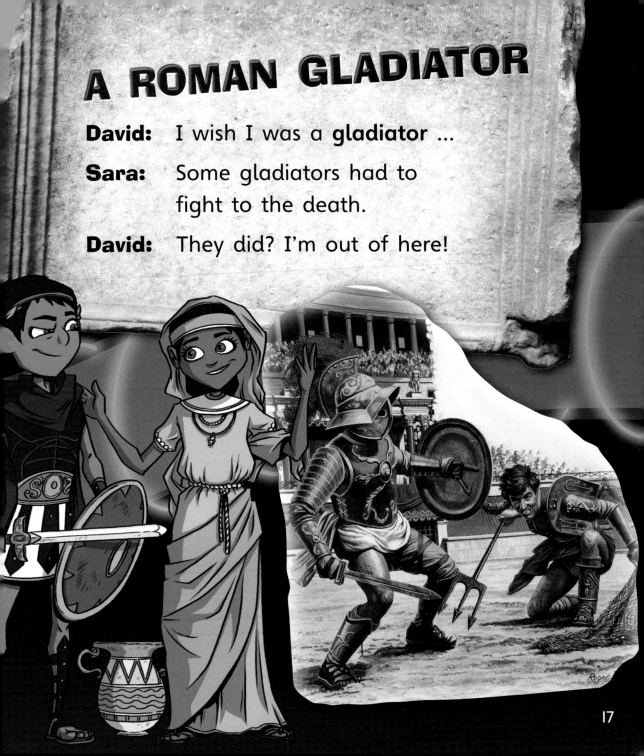

The Romans built straight roads to link places together. They also built amazing buildings.

This is what the Colosseum looks like today. Gladiator fights were held here.

THE ROMAN ARMY

Sara: Look! The Roman Army!

David: The straight road is great for marching along!

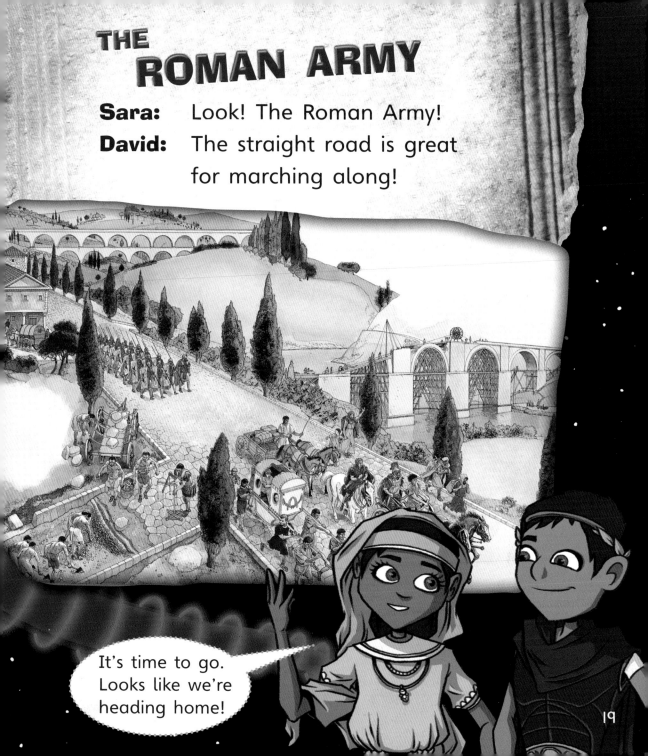

It's time to go. Looks like we're heading home!

GOING BACK AGAIN!

David: That's the end of our trip back in time.

Sara: I wonder what the ancient people would think if they came to *our* time?

David: Hmmm... Let's go back and ask them.

An Ancient Quiz

How much can you remember?

1 Where did Roman Gladiators fight?

2 Why was the Great Wall of China built?

3 What does the Sphinx look like?

4 What did Stone Age people eat?

Answers

1 The Colosseum

2 To keep China safe

3 The body of a lion and the head of a king

4 Animals, plants and berries

21

An Ancient Timeline

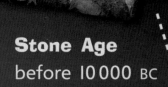

嗟又蕭條惡汁箐子穢愛妳
女云庭生秋汗不净头為粮食後
至五百万世頂騰爲鍊银之中
常起穢不净㳌斯吾厨之内
黑世勲者數千万劫无有出期
誰得酥脫痛不可言哀哉手窗場
林餅毘不得近厨食人肌之

Stone Age
before 10 000 BC

5 000 BC

10 000 BC

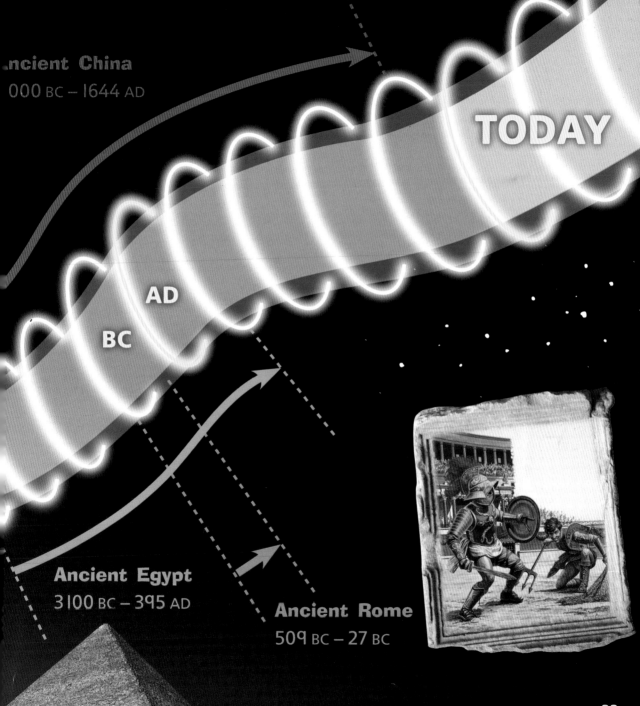

ncient China
000 BC – 1644 AD

TODAY

AD

BC

Ancient Egypt
3100 BC – 395 AD

Ancient Rome
509 BC – 27 BC

Glossary

ancient	very, very old
compass	tool showing directions such as north, south, east and west
invented	came up with an idea
gladiator	slave or professional fighter who entertained the public by fighting to the death
mummy	dead body that has been made ready for burial
pyramids	tombs for dead Egyptian kings and queens
statues	models of a person or animal made from wood, stone or metal